I0826300

Spoken Wordz

Edited by Audrey Liggins

Spoken Wordz

Interior Images: Annette Nena Balestier

Front Cover Design: Khiry Malik of The Magic Eye Photography Studios

Photography: Khiry Malik of The Magic Eye Photography Studios

ISBN-13: 978-0615654010 (Glover Lane Press)

ISBN-10: 0615654010

Also By Tina L. Cates A.K.A. Dyvacat

Kitty Kat Letters

The Mission of Glover Lane Press is to Uplift, Empower, Elevate the Masses and Provide American Jobs. Every book published by Glover Lane Press and it's many imprints, is printed and manufactured in the United States of America, ensuring and maintaining American employment.

DEDICATION

This book is dedicated to my two highest blessings, my children Raina and Xavier Cates. Push for your Dreams and they will Come True!!

Love Momma!

ACKNOWLEDGMENTS

This book took so many years, hours,& seconds in the making. The writing and editing over and over again was a toil but one of love. I realized that just as you groom your children and guide them in the right path, that is what Spoken Wordz had become for me, actual Birth!! I hope those who read this book gain some insight, challenge their history, find humor as well as a visual enjoyment.

Thank You My Jesus Christ, Lord & Savoir for being the cornerstone of my life!

I would like to thank Glover Lane Press for making this project happen! Thanks go out to all of my supporters who have pushed me time and time again to make this dream come true! Thanks to my Mother, Shirley Phillips and brothers Rodrick and Eldred Reid for being right there loving and inspiring me. Thanks to Lezlie Uko, Ernestine Heard, Johnson Uko Jr. and George Uko for being my extended family an embracing us with warmth and love. Thanks to my two little ones, Raina and Xavier Cates for being the loves of my life!! Thank you to my multitude of beautiful friends &

acquaintances I've met in this wonderful lifetime! You have truly been my Inspiration!

Special shout-outs to Leondra Charity, Anthony Blakely, Trescha Haley, Rachelle Armstrong, Elizabeth Cruz, Vicki Stephens-Allen and Alesia Atkinson! Your friendship means the world to me! Thank You several times over!

Thanks to Khiry Malik of The Magic Eye Photography for the cover design, Tonya Primus my Make Up Artist and Lil' Sis, and Annette 'Nena' Balestier for your fantastic Artistry and really making this come to Life!!

I Love You All for everything you are in my spirit!

Tina Cates

Dyvacat

Spoken Wordz

Author: Tina L.Cates

Poet Dyvacat

CONTENTS

Free

I feel free roaming softly in the dust
I danced circles around myself
it is so amusing
I feel Unstuck
no longer bound
just free
the melody my heart plays
no longer sounds the same
it has changed
and so have I
reaching beyond words
to find what waits for me
anticipation....anxiety
no matter what this life's
trouble brings to me
I'm free
no longer imprisoned
loved and lost and loved again
like an unspoken ritual pulled out
plucked
removed, released

Free!

Spoken Wordz

Once upon a time...

I laughed at the death of my very own existence
clueless, unknowing
unsure of what's really at stake.
See I built my fate on broken dreams.
Was raised on fairytale fantasies....
But PLEASE release me from those scribes,
written as stories for children
but STILL no answers to the question of... WHY?
Why can harm come to a little girl in this world?

You See...
Unprotected & harmed.... she alarmed her mother and father
but they didn't bother.
So abused, misused, and taken
made in secret & shaken to piercing eyes and premature penetration
that left her looking for love in that same old way.
And even though she thought that sex was just a word you say,
they still took her innocence anyway!

Now she's fast, shaking her
full-grown ass, but merely a teen
as she switched down the street

to some other old niggah
who she thought loved her
because of his whispered obscenities.
He wanted to take her hand and her candy too,
and baby girl already knew:
and knew just how to
twist her hips a bit,
bite her bottom lip an inch,
and hold her pert tits high to his pitch.
Now he's taken her bait...
after several days he would only masturbate
while she would wait patiently for her statutory rape!

I mean who's to blame besides the men?
When the media shows young girls how to shake their asses at them!!
And a 13 year old can find on the internet how to play footsies under the table with
someone else's husband??!!
And she always looked older than her age; at least that's what they said.
(I guess to justify what was going on in their heads...)
To take away more of her innocent world.
Thoughts of Cinderella and Snow White,
stuff she grew up reading but never quite understood.
The child gets older and allows her flesh to stretch

into unimaginable proportions.
Looking close to pregnant but never had an abortion.
See the pussy was too fast, the sperm couldn't take.
Barren, old, & fat... is that her fate?

She gorges on carbs,
loves them all from breads to pastries.
You can find her smiling most convincingly in all the best bakeries.
She reaches sizes 20...24...& even at times 26.
Thick in ass and hips,
she still has the nerve to switch.
Because Sex is still an addiction...
and not knowing how to be faithful,
she condemns herself in her own body's prison
pondering between food, sex, and complacencies,
And behold out of the mist of this confusion
God blesses her with ...
2 Beautiful babies??
Miracles are truly spiritual indeed!

Still immature but learning more,
She wants to give them
everything that she's still longing for!
Wants to protect and love her little boy
and teach him to ALWAYS respect each & every little girl!!

Want to get a shot gun out about her little girl!!
Teach her that hugging just may be okay but never ever more!
See the cycle can no longer turn anymore!!
As she frees herself from sex-addiction,
Trying through faith to escape her body's prison.
Feeling like fate should only teach
as she preached this speech to reach all the hurt babies!
Realizing that the past doesn't have to be her future.
And to shed those unwanted pounds,
not being afraid to be focused or even let down!
But to strive to be the best!!
And now that she wears an 'S' on her chest!!!
She remains humble because...
there are no promises for tomorrow.
It's called one day at a time!
And as she learns to hold her head up high,
gives herself permission to cry and
told herself to stop all the lies;
There is no longer sadness in her eyes.
And as she heals from the pain endured,
she realizes that sometimes she's just misunderstood,
But deep cuts do require sutures...
and she will no longer look in her Past
to predict or determine her Future!

The End

Poetry Slam Winner 2005, Found Theatre, Long Beach Ca.

Spear N2 Poetry Volume 2 Winner, 2012, Los Angeles Ca.

(You) Fancy Huh?

She walked in the room and everyone paused in order to take in her full elegance with that right touch of sass.

Her demeanor was subtle but confidence exuded from every pore.

She was aware of their awe because it happened everywhere she went.

"You Fancy Huh" was blasting down the street as a car passed by.

Sly smiles formed on unfamiliar faces as if they silently answered the question.

Her walk to the end of the room was uneventful for her but everyone else ... they whispered to each other

"Who is THAT?"

Some of them even felt they knew her and tried to recall if it was a TV show, movie, or some channel they seen her on before.

She herself just laughed inside about the stares she received that seemed to wonder down each and every curve her body produced.

She enjoyed this & made sure to walk just a little slower so they could really get a good look at what she was working with.

See last year at this time no one even as so much glanced in her direction.

At 350 lbs. she used the weight to hide herself... & she was successful.
Now with their gazes she knows that She IS strong enough, wise enough, Fierce enough and have lived long enough to take it all in....

and she does!

(You) fancy huh?

"You Damn Right!!"

The Last Letter I Wrote To My Man

Hello Mr. Black~

I finally decided to write this just to say a simple

'Thank You'
See you loved me so much, I just can't tell the World lies
that you were untrue!
You worshiped me with your words, enchanted by your
swerve, never once did I question your nerve.
Your approach was real, even told me how you feel and,
you always remained a gentleman in my presence;

I never had to gossip with my girls about you being an
adolescent
No,

You were a true man through and through, never once did
I ever doubt you
Still I have these words now to say to you ~
Yes the love you gave me amazed me
Drove that poor little 'straight' girl crazy, loved when you
called me "Baby"

Now there's only Maybe ~
Maybe in another life I will find you again
Because right now you can only be my best friend
See I've come to the realization that my identity was not
true
That I was unclear of what I was chosen to do, that's why I
can say I... no longer love you

See when I saw HER… there was NO Other
I loved her more than You, My Nubian brother
Watched her walk by with a seductive smile
Wide hips, big lips, sexy dip, driving me wild
Unclear what this meant, my curiosity pressed on
But she was like Me singing my favorite Ol' School song!!
Sure as hell didn't feel wrong!
As she guided me into the real of what was to come,
She imprisoned my body with kisses that had me sure enough sprung
We rubbed bodies, bumped coochies, kissed her passionately
Shared stories of what and how it used to be, she never ONCE questioned my identity
Time just pressed on, and sure enough from you I moved on
Now with the transition and process the Black Woman became MY realization
Of course now loving only her mental penetration!
She gave me the real Libation of Life
Damn society, *HOW COME SHE CAN'T BE MY WIFE!*

We share our world now co-mingled as one
We share my daughter and son
Living a fairy tale love song…
We laugh at times of what you see
She tells me that I'm the epitome of all her best dreams

So see there is no longer you~ my brother
For my Black Queen has now become MY Reality!

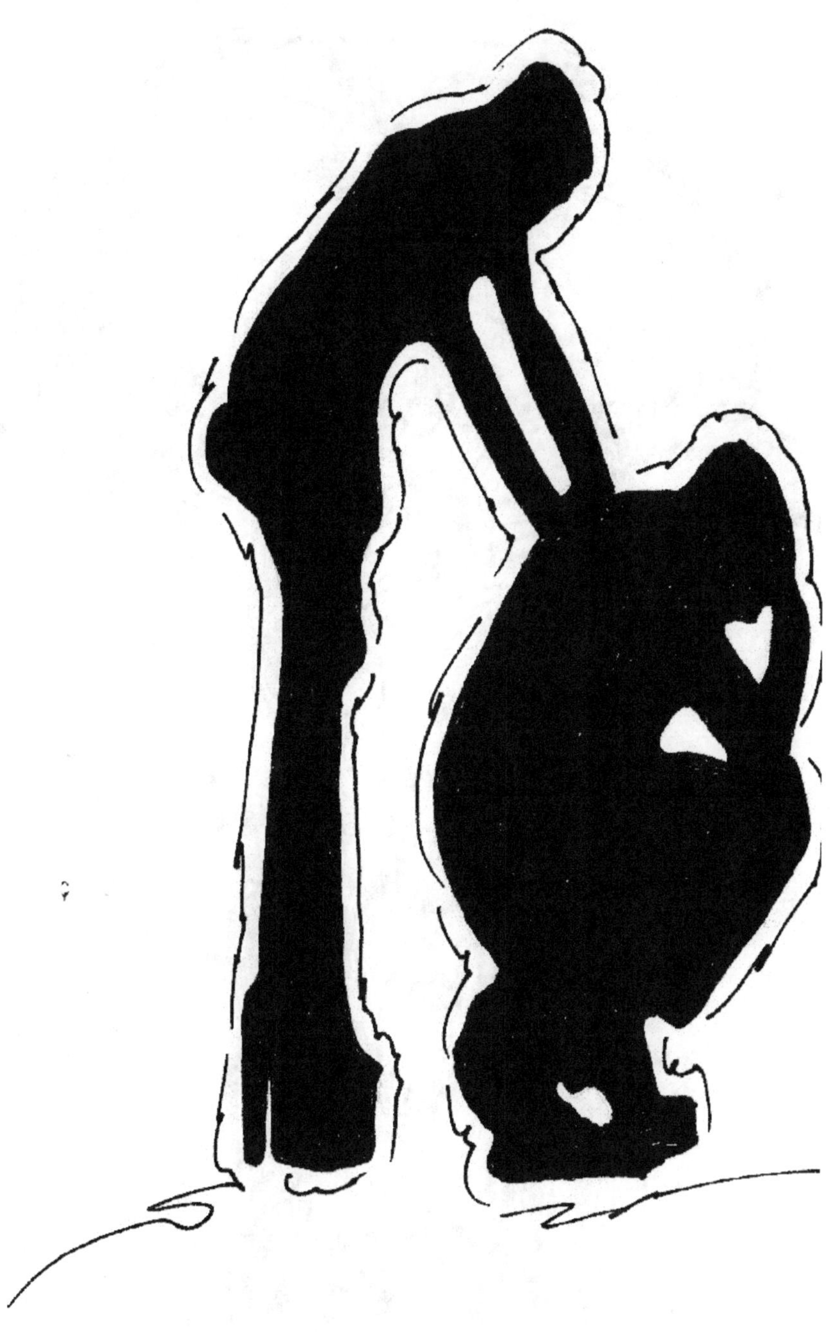

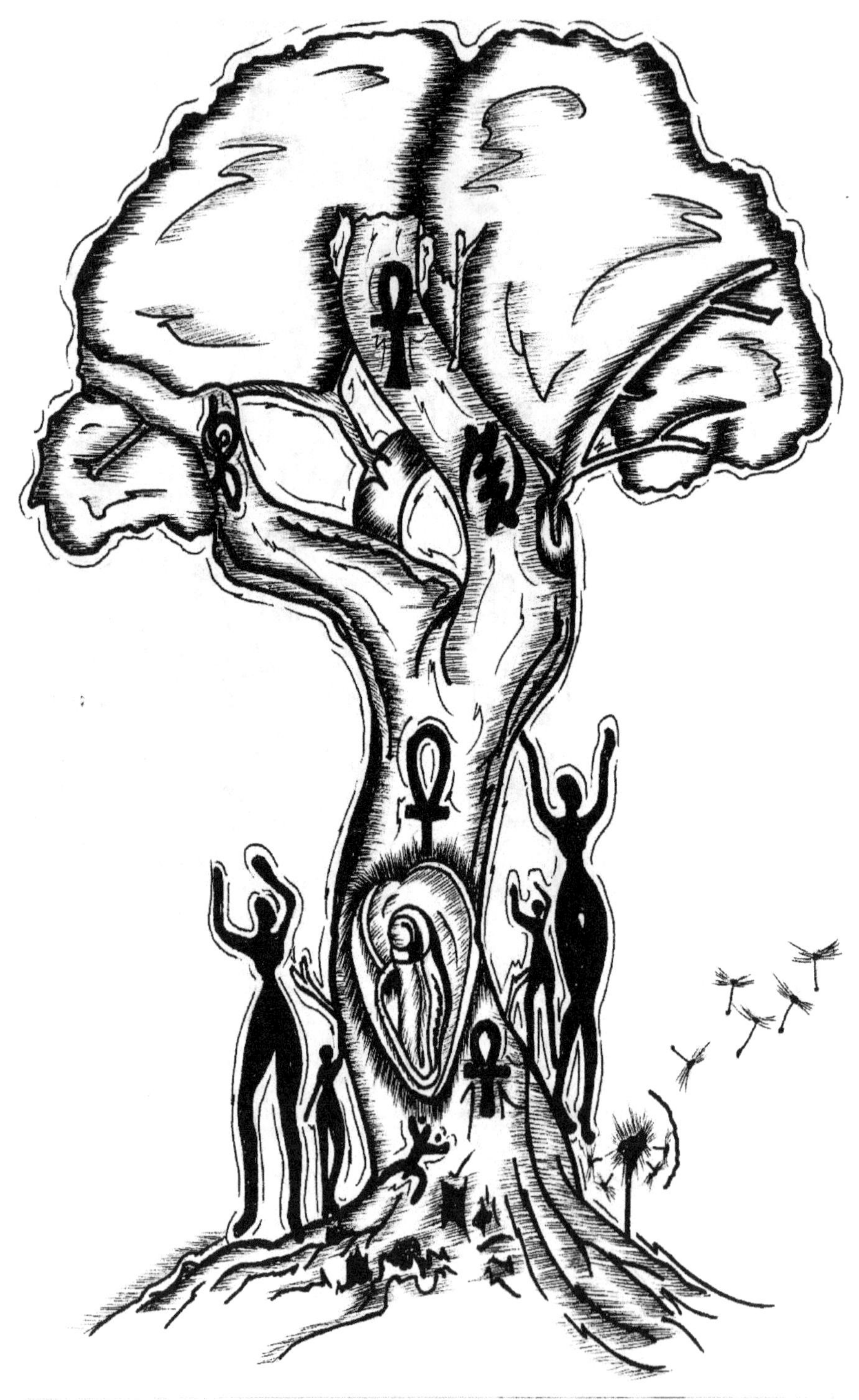

The Evolution of the Black Clitoris

1600's~ Africa

They call me "Your Highness"

Queen I am

I dance freely to drum beats

Hips swaying, moving rhythmically

I am a beauty for all to behold

Adorned in the finest of gold

Breast kissed by the warm Sun's glow.

Head held high...

I am free

But not from the ancient custom that awaits me...

It say the men's upset about our forbidden skin

The flesh's so big they won't be able to get in

It can hang so low they won't be able to make other

Men like them

Now Girls like me no longer Queens

We lay down by trees

as rituals scrape us clean

Female Circumcision is what they will call it in the States

But for me it's my tribal fate

Unable to walk proudly as before

I don't know how to hold my head up high in low times

See... Some of my Sisters died from this jealous curse

As for me I.... I no longer feel as beautiful as I once did

As I secretly touch the hardened scar that was once my Womanhood.

<u>1700's~ to the 1940's</u>

"WHERE DID THEY GO!!?"

"WHERE DID MY CHILDREN GO!!"

All Us women cry out

Folks runnin' left and right try'na get away

We watch our men bound by chains

Put us on ships to places we never knew existed

Twisted and scared

We lay bare and shown like cattle

to the next white man with the highest bid

Shoutin' "SOLD" now as we hid

trying to break free from the Masta's hand

My brothers be lynched in this new land

Us women be in sheds raped and savaged by the white man

left broken with no identity of the parts we were able to keep from the Motherland!

Strange Fruit... but Stranger silence as our men watch us make Mulatto babies that don't even look like us.

Ashamed as hands touch the pain in between

Our legs...

<u>50's & 60's</u>

Free at last Free at LAST!!

Martin Say

Equal Rights put up a mighty fight

No more slaves, no more chains

Promised 40 acres an a mule

Shoutin' bout our freedom

Yet I feel abused

My identity in shock

Ripped of my beauty

See they say we ugly

U can hear'um whispering

"Look at them Big ol' lips

Big ol' hips

That Big ol' nose'

"Where they come from who knows"

for me....

I know when I touch that

stiff nub between my legs under the covers

I make myself feel reeeaaal good!

And Beautiful

Shhhh...Nobody knows but God

<u>1960's</u>

Flower Child I Am

I am sassy, not caring to much about being classy

Held down by my dark skin

Yet again I need dollars to make sense

And I'll be damned if I work as a maid like my mother

And I'm sure not cut out to be no nurse!!

Drug induced prostitute is what they said

Shit hummph, not to concerned about that bull shhhhh

My next trick will be here soon

One more hit Baby!...... and I'm through

Let my mind take me to the Moon......

Laying on my back unaware of the treasure

I hold between my thighs

Being penetrated by this unknown tricks dick

all for my next hit

free?

Ohhh no not me

The 70's started the next revolution

((((((IT WILL NOT BE TELEVISED!!!))))))))

Shit the media lied and still kept us from knowing the pride

between our legs

Hosed down and pistol whipped from fits of outright rage

Not equip to undertake what had been taken

Black fist raised high despite the oppression.

Old black shacks with homemade fried chicken and collard greens in the background

Swinging back and forth and croon' in to the radio and old 8 tracks

He take me upstairs, lays me down

And does his business

He moans... I moan

He does his business

He moans and I....

He Does his business, moans, shakes and wails

Pulls up his pants and leaves

Well I'll be damned!

What about me?

<u>1980's</u>

Sassy & Classy

I walk down the street

Never know which man or woman I'm going to meet

Disco music at Studio 54

Donna Summer and Perms no more Afros

I'm so hot to trot forgetting where my ancestors came from

I mean who's to blame

I'm doing what I want to, right?

It is My Body we're speaking of!

AIDS hits the block but it won't get me….

Hmm mmm mmm that's what I thought a few years ago

as my Nurse unknowingly pulls hard on my IV.

I let my gift slip away by letting it loose like change

as I watch my final line display

beeeeeeeeep………………

<u>1990's</u>

Resurrected, I'm no longer infected

Safe Sex or Abstinence are the choices that keep me protected.

It's the coming of Age and the craze is Satisfaction

Women put down if they want to get down

Men still hold the crown

Everything geared all towards them

Your clitoris?? I'm not putting my tongue on that!

No response just a shy grin.

Left us pleasure less.

Until we discovered our second best as

fingers found that special bud

we rubbed ourselves into the next generation

of full-on Masturbation

<u>2000</u>

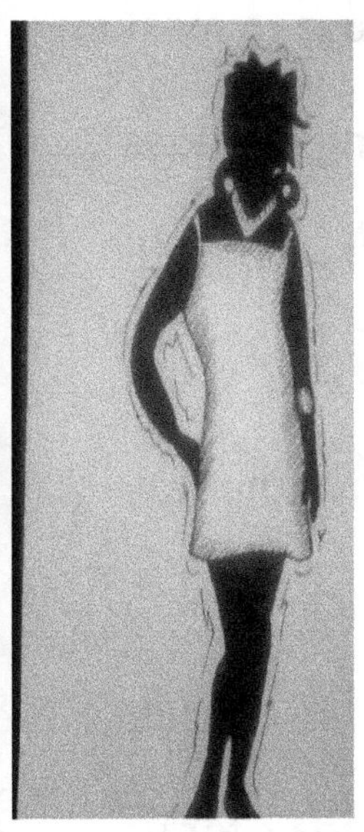

Today we play and tell of what we do

Especially after the AIDS plague chose us, too

The Clit no longer that hidden Taboo

Toys, stimulants, and books now hooked

We celebrate our womanhood

We scream about it in poems

Sing about it in songs

Testify to our girlfriends how we had the dick of Kong!!

We're watched when we walk down the street

Our lips, hips, and butts are the desire of Society

Major cash loot found in rump shaka' beauties bouncin'

those heavenly big asses on the hottest scenes,

makin' it rain on Music videos played all day long on TV

Even our "thickness" has become a prosperous commodity

as you see big boned African-American Sistahs grace the covers of the most lavish magazines

But not to mention, Oprah Winfrey has become a Mentor and Muse to most

And not to boast, you know that saying still goes

'Once you go black, You won't go back!!'

We can be proud for we have come a long ways.

Authors like Zane & Ilyana Vanzant still pave the way

We EVEN have a Beautiful Black Woman

as America's First Lady!!

This is dedicated to us for us

I Celebrate Our Black Womanhood

Our Beautiful, sacred mounds are revolutionary

Hail to the Black Clitoris!!

Let the Evolution Continue!

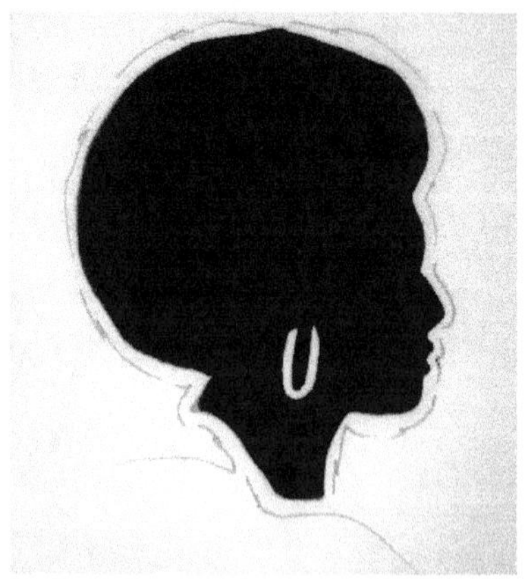

POOL OF LOVE

Let me submerge myself into your abyss
Diving my heart mimicking a Professional into your pool of emotions
Your realm releases all tension as you sustain me
I survive only with the breath found in your whispers
I welcome the taste of saltiness in your tears as I kiss your lips
Allow me to sink further than anyone else
Into your 'unknown' where secrets are hidden from even yourself
Open your Ocean~part it like the Red Sea
I feel the land at the bottom, which is of your soul~
Shout, 'Behold' warning me that your waves want to crush.
I can feel some resistance, but I submerge further and your fears hush
You allow me to explore your other Worlds and some of your past lives
All of your doors open as you watch me adapt to this new existence
I have taken on a position in your future, in your life
Without land or air, my love is persistent and doesn't succumb to any wear or tear
You have shielded me with your armor

I love how you flow through me and begin to make my words the air you breathe

Lost in space I see the glow of your face as you make your presence known in my own Deep-Sea
I have become accustomed to loving you...~

Ohhh, the Beautiful sights I see as I bask in your Ocean!

Coming Home Again

My home is with you
nothing other in the World will do for me
See…
Imagined dreams point to you
It's utterly true
they do!
Fears try to appear and make me feel
like I'm locked in a cage
Enraged…
I want to come out
In doubt really for no reason at all
See…
You never stalled or balled screaming
"We're through!"
Never once walked away when I tired to embrace you
You remained true to me
And I see where my peace lies…
in your eyes
I find myself relaxed
In fact…
Your love to me is tranquil
Graceful
Even…
Spiritual
All my fears cease
and I'm able to release myself fully onto you
My once imprisoned heart consumes you

Taking you All
In…
Your perfections…objectives….
And even old bullshit resurrected
Or thoughts infected
Completely unconditional
Because even in your worse days
My World is at peace when I'm with you
It's all utterly true
And soon….
I will bask in your eyes again
Exhale again
Breathe…
Yet
Again
Be Home Again

70's Grove Thang

I'm that Black Panther Princess
Trying to get in yo business
Are you with this?
I'm talking to you
Yeah you
Sweet thang
Sportin' that psychedelic pantsuit
and the leather boots
Got that funky afro
freshly picked out
Got my mind grooving to how those hips switch
from left to right
My Flower child
you sure are... (hand clap) Dy-no-mite!
Can I pick you up in my deuce and a quarter tonight?
We can go to that hip club down on 1st
where the sounds are groovy
Or what about a drive-in movie?
I'm just asking you out on a date?
Promise not to bring you home too late
I know that would be a mistake
Shoot, I just need you close girl
Can you dig it?
Right On....
I knew you feel it!
Foxy Sista
You mean in those jeans!

Would you wear them for me tonight?
Or how about that skinny mini skirt
that makes me wanna flirt with you
when I'm not even trying to!
Girl you look out of sight
in those afro puffs
silver eye shadow and lip gloss!
Or the hot pants on with the high boots
So fierce!
Baby girl I'm Serious!
I just need to get with you
We can cruise on up to the point while I play my 8 track
coming on strong like the Mack
Try'na get to first base...
Baby Girl, I just really need to see how your Bubble gum taste!!

So Sista...

What's Hap'nin'?
Can this girl take you out...
And Groove with you tonight?

Fusion OutFest Sabor 2005

Screaming Whispers...

A girl out of breath, panting, exhausted

Vulnerable to that cry within. Screaming loudly out of jealousy and insecurities.

Not aware that she was being manipulated by that demon that laid dormant inside of her.

Fits of rage escapes her broken heart, striking blows at her lover who only knew abuse anyways.

See her woman grew up with a mother that knocked her head off on a daily....

"So this is how you show me you love me. You Love Me don't you?!"

"I ....DO love you"

My soul open wide, being everything but nothing at the same time.

The bully was in my mind as the rage took control.

No longer the gentle lover I knew before. Transformed me into an unknown I dare not know.

Controlled by my emotions, unable to even see as before.

PRAYING to GOD please! "What if she says this or that, call me a bitch, call me fat...

You Fat Bitch!!!..

Ouch!!

It called out loudly, striking bones and marrow to the core.

Bloody rivers of my puddles from words said by my lover.

More lashes from lips that once tasted like sweet dripping honey dew melon,

now salty with hatred and venom.

Blow by blow it seems to never end.

Rage escapes!

A shoe thrown from the other side of the room crashes into the cocktail table,

mind shouts “WHY can’t we ever keep shit!!”

Terror, as if in slow motion.

Clock ticking

When will this end?

Fast forward to the next day,

finding her in kitchen wearing an apron cooking eggs???

What is this Mess!!!

Me waking up ashamed, exhausted and hurt.

Actually seeing her the victim thinking, Maybe this thing can work?

More prayers,

More good days with her.

The lay down real good, the stand up unnatural bullshit...

but I never quit.

Still more growing to do.

The last encounter of the ugly kind was just an alibi for her to hit the streets.

Instead hitting the floor and a new introduction to the 4 B's:

Bitter words, Blows, Busted lips, and Bruises.

Silently whispering, It has to stop, love doesn't feel like this!!

Only seeing bits and pieces of how abusive it really is.

A day away where lessons are learned.

Contemplation, reflection, the truth un-scorned.

Picked up the one thing that I learned....

The end of this would only wind up in Prison, Hospital, or the Morgue.

Screaming whispers of words that changed my life,

still knowing that HE's not done yet with my life.

Whispering

"You are only in control of your Response! You are only in control of YOUR Response! You are ONLY IN CONTROL OF YOUR RESPONSE!!'

I got it!

Tested in the worst way when one long night she was ready to fight.

Started the lashes, the fat asses, the whole act so I would give in like I used to.

Trying to scurry up hatred and anger, she was down-right evil.

"Not this time"... Peace began to enter me traveling through my bones... "Not this time!"... Serenity circulated through my blood & touched each limb.... "Not this time!!!"... "HE shelters me with HIS blood!!"

This time My bully won't win.

Looking at her closely, this person I loved was unfamiliar.

As if looking at her through a glass, I felt no longer imprisoned.

More words thrown but they didn't hurt anymore.

My bully didn't win, as her own rage grew stronger within.

Wanting me to turn into something I was not....

And I'm Not,

and will never be again!

Hearing old folks say "Baby, Bullies aren't born they're made!"

The terror that once made itself a friend to strike back was intact.

No longer living in fear of the verbal abuse that made me snap!

Made new decisions on what I expected.

And one of my very first rules is

No kind of Crazy will EVER be accepted.

Screaming Whispers...

Excerpt from *Letters to My Bully*, 2012

Freedom in She

I found a new freedom
Freedom I tell you!
Something more spectacular than this day-to-day routine
World we live in
A freedom in...

Well, a Freedom in *She*
She can see though me, you know
Eyes penetrating my flesh that interrupts my thoughts
My heart pounds for a breath of clear air for lungs that
just may stop short of a last gasp
Layers are removed as my soul opens up to her
It's that type of Freedom Y'all!

A freedom in *She*

I remember when I first picked up the pen to write about
her,
It was like an actual calling for me to express the reasons
why I love her like I do
I wanted to tell the truth, share my inner most thoughts
And realized quickly... that nothing in any written
language could describe it fully
I mean it was something about that smile that caused me
to pause
and that same smile that continuously allows me to rest
all my fears and insecurities

into her heavenly abyss... and with bliss became a sea of emotions only revealed in my secrets

It was that Freedom, I tell you

That freedom in *She*

When I submerge myself into her whims, skillful hands find their way to a warm, wet, wicked core as fingers enjoy their newfound habitat setting free her waves upon waves of convulsions
Sometimes it's like the Earth stands still (pause) just to be seduced her cries of passion

Mm mm mmm
Hey I got that *'It'*
You know that *'It'* that makes you smile all crazy and shit!
That *'It'* that caused an involuntary twitch from that sexual fit you had the night before!
That *'It'* that makes your heart bleed and weep, and for some of you even Creep...
I mean, whatever is clever!

My pen lost its stroke until I took that toke and wrote about her
Daze in a haze it never left the page
I mean love poems ran frantically in my brain
Time stood still as each syllable was formed

I was writing shit like ‘I never knew love could be this good or this sweet before”

and now in her love I have been set free
as she called to me and I answered making myself her love sacrifice
and in return I’ve been given satisfaction without really even asking for it.

I’ve been set free Y’all

A freedom in....

Well...A Freedom in *ME*!

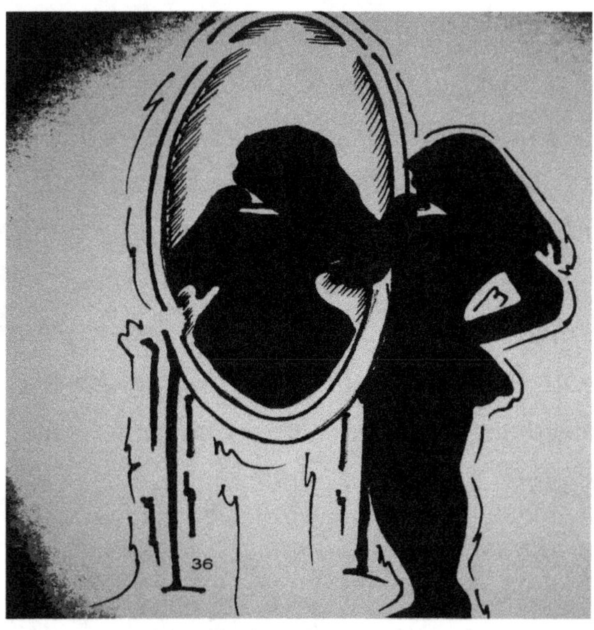

Poetry Slam Winner, 2005 Found Theatre, L.B. CA.

Laugh Again

I wish I could take the rain clouds that storm over your head alone and make them go away longer than a few minutes, an hour or a day. Tell it to leave you alone, remove it from your home and see you laugh again.

Oh how I love the way you laughed! It was robust, loud, and made everyone in its presence laugh as well just to be a part of its delightfulness.

Now there is no more. Standing tall, but slumped over from toil and labor while life shoots blows at you. People all say it could be worse but, what is worse than feeling like no one could understand or even withstand what you're holding in your heart like a diseased mound of scarred flesh. You hold it in only corroding even the good parts of you. It's hard to hold the outer together when the inner is withering away from life's maddening decay. Pain nauseates the head and poisons the mind. We all have lessons to learn, some harder than others, and that all too familiar saying, 'It all gets better in time'

What will it take to make you laugh again?

Laugh openly, wholeheartedly and freely?

Baby, I want you to know that

I am Here

I Am Here

I AM HERE

Here to make you smile, to listen to your cries, to understand the pain, to ease the rain. To nourish you, protect you and shelter you from harm. To stand beside you arm in arm.

My Love...Please

LAUGH AGAIN!!

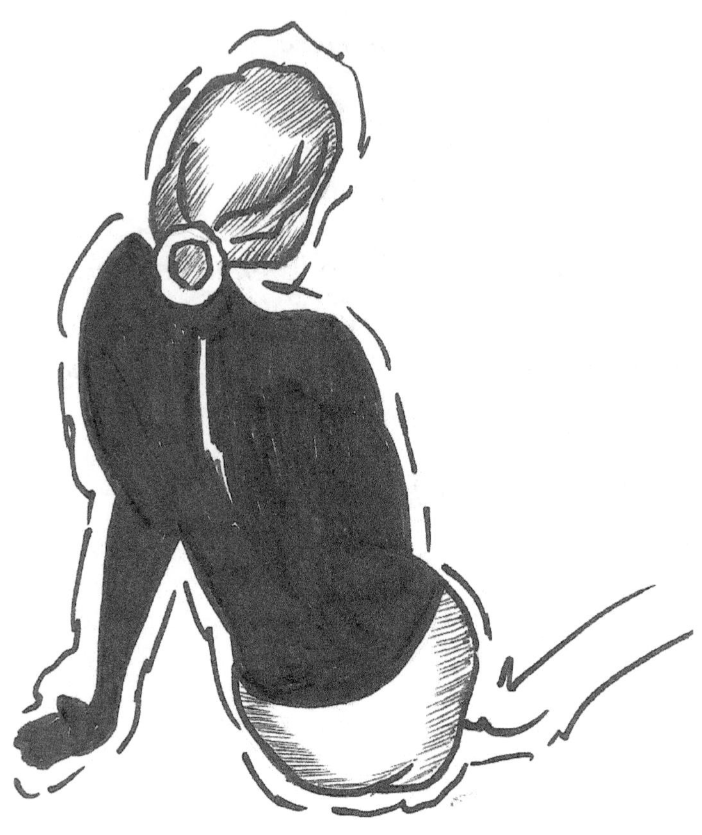

12.23.11

They told me you didn't have to wake up...

They said when it burst you could have went to sleep and never come back!

But the Lord and I wasn't having that!!!

There is no Way, No way in Hell you should ever be taken from me

No way that no one could ever make it clear for me to see

If something like that were to happen to you,

my heart would live for an eternity in fear!

See... I love you so much...

and with all the stress, blood pressure and stuff

It just burst, busted, blazed into your brain

Left stains with pains that can't erase times past

ICU sheets instead of being home with me and your family

Baby I love you!

And I wish there was a way I could get through to you, to let you know

We gotta stop this never-ending cycle of time,

where we push ourselves for that nickel and dime
Only not to understand the truth
That not only do we live and strive for personal pursuits
But for the love of our family and friends
Baby they came through and still coming through
Praying to our Lord, Our Father above
Telling HIM please let her stay
For 1-2-3 more days, months, years, lifetimes, ages
Praying to be by her side, her lover, her friend
To let her know we can get through anything
This world pushes, plummets, and piles upon us
As Long as HE holds us
Nothing can stop us
Thank You Father for seeing another Day!

Know My Name

A world of lifeless melodies
blocked like sunshine behind dark clouds
These are what unmet needs are.
Eyes clueless to what's right in front of you.
Seeing but being blinded
asking for mysteries to unfold
but...
can it be the truth that I actually seek
or is it some small answer into the type of occurrence that
causes heartbreak when dreams are not met?
Well my questions only lie in the hands given to me at birth.
My plowing of the Earth to unfold what lays before me
knowing that it is actually in HE that things come.
My plan~ (only if He says the same)
is to know my Name!

Let it ring with ease, simple praise, love, and miracles for
myself & others.
Let it bring joy and laughter to those no longer able to sing.
Make warm smiles shine like diamonds against the light!
But only if... He says the same!

In actuality, He has given me all these things

and things I wondered why He felt I deserved them.
I found that seeking is easy if we seek in that 'direction'

That direction that WILL unfold the truth to you.
Frustration comes when Faith is absent
so I lean toward the Faith that sustains my sanity my...
fears in this life, my fears of an unfair World.
Unfolding is the plan
The plan that only comes from letting go
moving...driving...wanting
"wanting" (pause)
That word is nothing to be ashamed of
Wanting brings about the Need for all things.
I learned that the hard way~
Wanting is what life is made of

And my want
Is to know my Name!

Let it ring with ease, simple praise, love, and miracles for myself & others.
Let it bring joy and laughter to those no longer able to sing.
Make warm smiles shine like diamonds against the light!
But only if... He says the same

Hip~Hop Dee 1985

A tribute to the untold stories of Hip Hop

She rocked Hip-Hop to the break-a-break-a dawn
Mad if someone announced her name wrong
She was what you call 'funky fresh' upon the mic
Her lyrics were tight, and she always kept the crowd hyped!
She wrote track tricks that flipped & dipped into mellow hip hop beats
Then have the crowd jump to their feet when she had her DJ flip the beat!!
She ran circles over all the other female rappers that became more famous than she
But the masses was never blessed with her rhythms
You could only buy her cassette tapes at underground venues to hear them
They didn't understand her, although she could handle the mic
They just weren't impressed by her look and felt it just wasn't right!

Because....

She was a straight up Butch and you never had to guess
Cause in her hooks she would say 'She' instead 'It'
Or 'Her' instead of 'Him',
as she rocked baseball caps and Timbs.
Wore boxer shorts under sagging jeans just so you could see them.
They tried to change her ways so she could get paid
But she stayed away from that lie

Even her homeboy manager tried, and she fired him on the spot!
Got mad when the industry past her by with a 'NOT!!'
She still managed to make it to those funky clubs
where all the ladies and fellas showed her much love.
Her tapes bumped down the street in droves
as she made her money on the down low.
She continued to work hard to be exactly what her dreams were,
even though she was treated like a guest on Jerry Springer!

They liked her music but just couldn't see her!

She thought
“Maybe if I soften up they'll let me in the industry
where I should be! Shittt I'll still be me!
Maybe when I get paid and have it made
I could just go back to my old ways”
So out she went with make-up on, a cute little outfit
and fake nails on.
Looking at her it was hard to believe
I mean Ol' girl was even wearing a weave!
Sat down with some dude from the industry
He was impressed and wanted to see
So he took her to the studio to give it a try
She walked in confidently thinking "which one should I put down?"
She replaced the 'She' with 'He' and the 'Her' with 'Him'

Tried to make it appear that she was straight even though she wasn't
Justifying her behavior like everybody does it.
Things went well, started having countless record sells.
She even did a remake to LL's 'Rock the Bells'
She grew very famous and hit the charts
Made it to #1 with her song called 'My Private Parts'
In the video she shook her ass and showed her ass
all for the cash!
Men started looking trying to get with her
But she blew them away before they could diss her!

Years later still stuck in a lie,
she started contemplating suicide.
Her world was spinning entirely too fast
And the lyrics which were no longer hers, made her head for a crash
She started sniffing cocaine to ease the pain but that became an addiction
Even on the mic you could see ol' girl shaking & twitching
Then she started to drink more,
To deal with her New occupation: Crack Whore
The woman that stood by her side finally left her,
the transition was too much so she packed up the Benzo.
The drugs got harder and harder as she became smarter and smarter on how to get her next hit
Not the kind on the turntable,

but with a pipe you smoke with.
Started using record sells and royalties
to get high on crack cocaine and weed.
Soon she even got a case of VD
But tried to change her life when
she realized it could have been HIV!

She had no choice but to get paid
Put out 3 songs in just one day
But it was too late
She already breached her contract
Bailed out on 3 concerts without even making contact!
She was slowly moving down the charts
And prayed with fear and a broken heart!
Asked God for forgiveness in some kind of way
Asked for a sign that things will be ok.
She knew she needed some direction
And now without money, drugs, cars or affection
she had no choice but to believe in the Resurrection!
Sometimes she would walk down the street
And faintly hear her lyrics and tight beats.
"I know my mission is not complete, I know my mission is not complete!"
she would repeat
One day something came in the mail
that made her scream and yell.
It actually made her stand to her feet.

She tore the envelope open and read it repeatedly!
It was a party to honor her for who she was,
and changed herself in order to be heard
They had other artist who were also invited there
to see this musical rendition of her life's documentary!
The day came and she was running a little late.
Not sure of what to wear thinking maybe a dress will be ok
But then thought to herself 'Hell no! This lie will have to end!!'
So she reached in her closet and pulled out a pair of sagging jeans and checked out her Timbs!
Had her hair corn-rowed back with a touch of gel
Sprayed on some cologne designed especially for males
Wore NO 'Fake-Up' the term she had for Make-Up back then.
Went to the show straight "Butched" down!
Actually even tried to clown!
Cleaner than any man that came that day
Her Staci Adams shinning and sporting digs made by Fendi!
The press took pictures and asked a bunch of questions
She just smiled, nodded and entered in a different direction
Sat in the front row with her family
Loving the whole show, now coming to the grand Finale!
She watched the Dancers shake their butts
Seen the DJs spin real tuff
Watched the Rappers do their stuff
And R&B Singers press their luck

They announced her to come up and spit some shit.
Feeling fine as hell, pops her collar thinking, "I'm too legit to quit!!"
She grabs the mic and tells the crowd
“Thank You!!”
“For all these years I was never true to you,
But I appreciate each and every one of you!!'
The fans roar with screams of her name
No more of her being ashamed as
she rocked the mic that night with no hesitation,
even some of her underground stuff...
The crowd grew quiet just to listen.
Left them standing on their feet when she
replaced all the ‘Him’s to Her and the ‘He’s to ‘She!’
and "From now on," she shouted,
"That's the way it will always be!!"

The moral of the story is:
Don't ever compromise yourself or your art for a life in the Industry!!

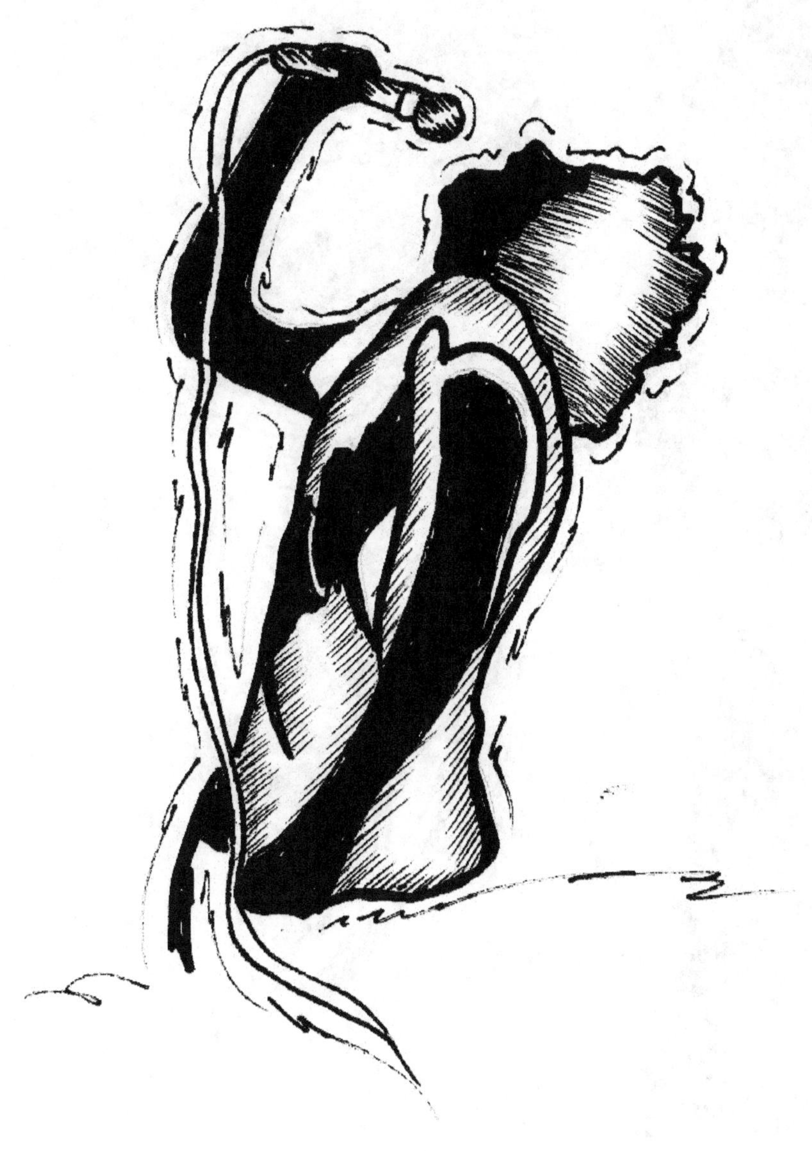

PAINTED ROSES

Melody~~~~

Painted Roses, Painted Rose, Painted Roses, Painted Rose, Painted Roses... Painted Roses...

Exposed were the thorns

I could not see... me

No longer hearing me

Found the thing that made it change

Clearly, Completely

I thought I knew, scared to see the truth

That Love Can Be True!

Trust in (wo)man, my heart, my love, my hand and other parts I couldn't withstand.

Now I see.. what grew in me

Painted Roses, Painted Roses, Painted Roses... yeah

Beauty from the outside comes from within

Yet again I sinned 3 or more times with my friend

I'm not perfect in anyway

My purpose was not to stray

Yet is comes swiftly, fiercely

And now I suppose, you may think I'm a hoe

If you see it that way, believe it that way

Love changes like time and rain

Stained on the inside

Stained on the outside

Thorns are blazed, excite the pain

The heart wants to stray

Now I see... the feeling in me

Supersedes all rationality really

Painted Roses, Painted Rose, Painted Roses, Painted Rose, Painted Roses... repeat

The suit of armor I had over me

Dissolved so fairly and quickly

I was almost back to the old me but...

Knowledge is Freeing

Knowledge is freeing me

No longer succumbing to this or that

Unless I know the facts

Unless I want to get this thang tapped

Knowledge is Freeing

Knowledge is freeing me

But I'm good right now

The power of will and know how

I'll try my best to past this test

To beat this shit from off my chest

Painted Roses...Painted Roses... Painted Roses...Painted Roses... *Painted Roses, Painted Rose, Painted Roses, Painted Rose, Painted Roses... Painted Roses...*

HERE

Finally
You are Here
Here as my token of past broken hearts
Here as my lesson on life as it relates to love
Here as my gift of accomplishing a mission of loving myself
At my most vulnerable state
Naked and striped away
You are Here
How fortunate I am

I am Here
To provide to you everything I've learned about loving you in the right way
Here to give you all of what's good at my humblest state
Here to erase the negative fates of yester-year
Here to clear your path in my life
Unconditionally and lovingly
I am Here
How fortunate you are

We are Here
To give all the love needed because we both deserved and earned it!
Here to provide trust needed to sustain and hold us close
Here to share all that the Most High has given, taken away, and given back several times over!

Here

To begin a chapter of life, love, laughter, and love some more.
Here to provide one full of knowing who and what we are presently
Here to flourish Spiritually which only strengthens what we do share.
Here to give and receive
Give and receive
Give and receive all of which we are and still becoming!
Finally here to learn the lessons of love equipped with what we already know and understand of ourselves

We are Finally Here.... You & I

How Fortunate We Are!!

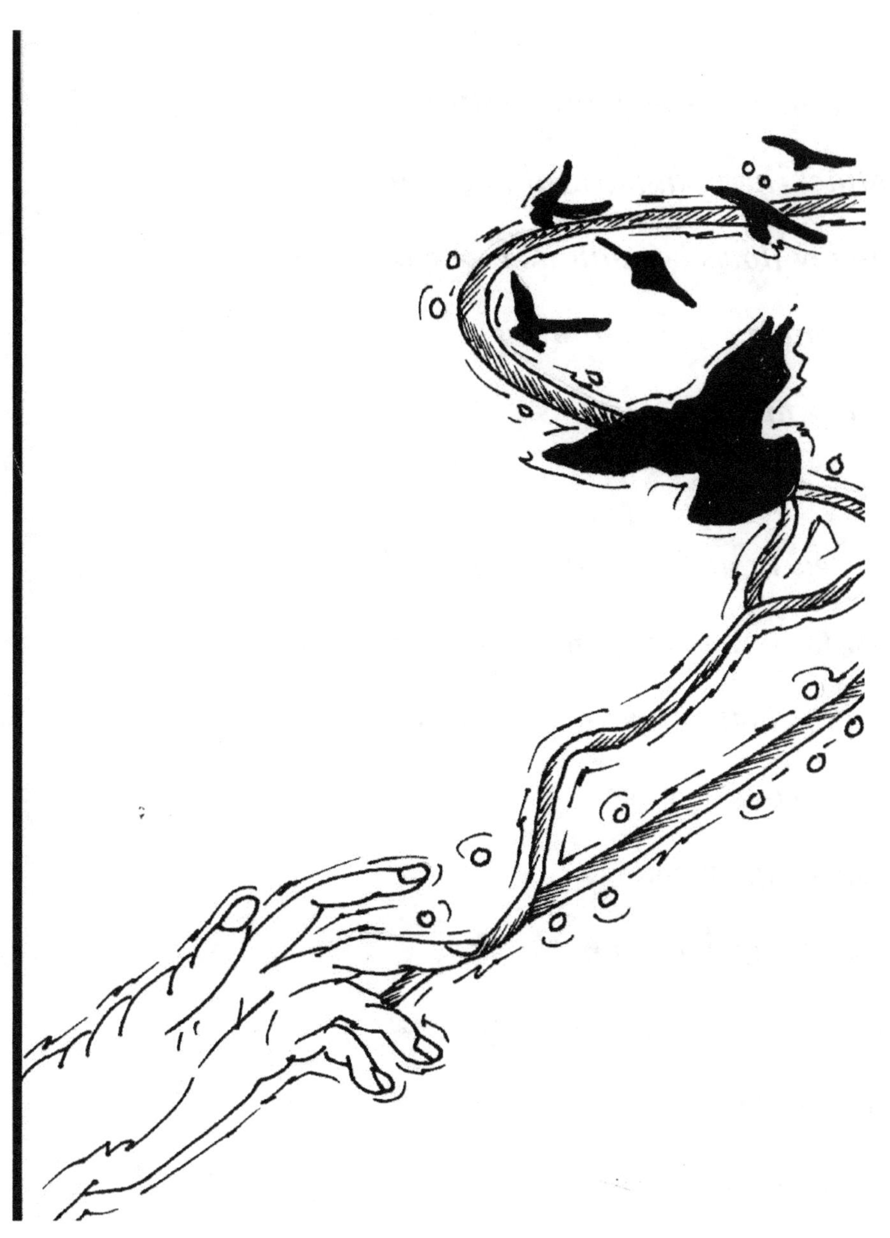

energy

you move through me swiftly

attacking with painful passion

honey flows beneath us like electricity

the energy is astounding

move me

you do

the earth and time are confused

birds flying south make their way toward us

this is hotter than any summer can get!

wet, wicked, free

touching or not

the energy has us

tantric lovers in a past life

not sure of how far it goes

shaking in orgasmic waves tempting to blow us

overboard

just from the touch of her hand

...Or not

Steel Drum

My heart beats to the rhythm of a steel drum
Pounding mercifully into a state of consciousness
The drumming is sometimes filled with aches and sorrow
Yet sometimes the percussion will find joy and love
Methodically each beat is played
At times it will include the snare
and accolades from popular symbols
My heart beats to the sound of the steel drum
Mind boggling thoughts that can keep it at a spastic rhythm
Piercing the flesh with each clash (smash!)
Life and its circumstances sometimes wants to hog the drum
With no tune in mind, it bangs like a child at play
Love sometimes picks up the sticks
to play a beautiful beat
that can sexily seduce you into a dance

My family has its own tune
It's the sound of sweet support to all of life's banging
percussion
Friends share in the fun and laughter
the drums clash together in unison
like a finely tuned drum rendition
My heart beats to the sound of a steel drum
As the rhythm picks up with questions
It wonders...
Just how long do we all have to suffer
in an indecent World?

Why so much pain and sorrow?
Why so much famine and abandonment?
What about the sheltered or battered?
or the ones undeserving of fame?
My heart continues to beat to the rhythm of a steel drum
And hopefully when all is said and done
I will go in a blaze of Glory
When my symphony is played!

Blue Notes

(A Blue Note were notes played in low tones, also called the "worried" note in African-American History)

Blue notes made "Blues" notes back in the Jim Crow days, and even before when our ancestors were slaves:

Picking cotton in huge fields, thistles and thorns in finger tips, hearing the Field Hollers over the sound of cotton gins, across country roads there were imprisoned men working hard on chain gangs, given numbers no names, sang and chanted all to pass the time away.

Because

Blue notes made "Blues" notes back in the Jim Crow days, and even before when our ancestors were slaves.

The Masters put us in churches because they thought the black man was uncivilized, taught us about a blue eyed man named Jesus, Repenting for our sins, we wept and cried, separated by color, not even considered a man. Slavery and Forgiveness they tried to make us understand. From our strength and spirit Gospel born became our stand and took over African-American history till this present day. Spirituals like "Precious Lord" and "Amazing Grace", called us to pray for The Holy Ghost, Baptism, and Sanctity. The Church gave us Call and Response ~ Can I get and Amen, and the church says AMEN

Because

Blue notes made "Blues" notes back in the Jim Crow days, and even before when our ancestors were slaves.

Years go by as work songs sung all across country roads of Georgia to the Carolina's turned into the Blues, sung in old night clubs about work, toil, sex, and poverty. Harmonicas, pianos, guitars strung in perfect harmony, striking blue notes born from New Orleans. Jazz generated from blues and crossed over to the White man too. Amazed by its strength, they took lots of money by letting Pat Boone croon to our tunes. Jazz was born when folk music, ragtime and gospel met. Ragtime, Swing and Count Dixie's Band played those Jazz town blues. Can't forget Satchmo's cheeks when he blew....

Because

Blue notes made "Blues" notes back in the Jim Crow days, and even before when our ancestors were slaves.

Soul was introduced with the hottest artist Motown produced. Who can't forget the sounds of Smokie Robinson, Ashford and Simpson and the Mighty OJays!

Stepping into the 70's brought shows to us like Soul Train. The longest syndicated show on screen! Don Cornelius put black Artist on the stage that became a staple in everyone's home. Watching Marvin Gaye sing "Inner City Blues" and "What's Going On" live on TV, you had to scream loud so everyone knew it was on!! There was no party in the seventies and still some till this present day that the Soul Train Line didn't let you do your thang!!

That's also the year we stepped into the generation of Hip Hop, born in the late 70's in the Bronx. Some thought it was a fad, thought it wouldn't last. But the music took over all races, cultures and creeds. Gave minority youth an identity. Rose from poverty, made millionaires out of street hustlers with them street degrees. In the mixes you hear samples of music from the past. Jazz, Funk, Blues, and Soul, samples played over beats while Artist flowed. Sprouted from there came R&B and Neo Soul. Our music continued to cross all boundaries from country, pop and even opera,

Our Music

Our History!!

Because

Blue notes made "Blues" notes back in the Jim Crow days, and even before when our ancestors were slaves!

My Muse

There was a time she used to love me
enjoyed every single thing about me
would smile and wink
just flirt with me
She would read my poetry
decipher each story
even shared some of her own
Her first poem I printed
framed and placed in my home
I was inspired by this one I admired
Had given me 'that one thing' I needed
continually repeated
and when my poems would sing
she would see it
felt and let it seep into her bones
She knew It was no one else but her in my words
because they were her home
and in my joy I made it that way
like a child lost at play
rolling gently down a hill
she stood still and watched me
playing in flower petals
She just grinned
That's how her love is
And I walked proudly within it
held it deeply in my spirit
and wrote more

my Muse she was
So close to me I swore my heart beat inside of her
The breath she took released air from my lungs
Eloquent grace was always the case
in whatever we embraced
She was a Sassy Sistah
No one mistook her for anything less
Cause *girllll* the way she looked and dressed
she demanded nothing but the finest no less
and I was truly impressed
by her finesse
and the way she handled her shit
Confidence that couldn't be dealt with!
All of these things within her
and to top it all off
a genuine heart
what more could I ask of her
The time had come for us to say goodbye
She was hurt and so was I
when we parted I never had a dry eye.
Friendship preserved
I thank her for the opportunity
to have felt such unity
to be held divinely
in love
And spirituality

My Muse
Thank You

GIFTS

What would you do if you had a gift?
Something special HE blessed you with.
That thing that lets you bend & shift to your very own music?
What would you do if you had a gift?
Something to make a profit with?
To tell your stories to the World & share all the glory with.
What would you do with it?

What would you do if you had a gift?
Would you even know what it is
or what it meant?
Or even how to take the steps to make it succeed?
What would your gift be?

He's shown me my gift
It's to be a Poet.
It's stated in Psalms 139.
He knew even before I wrote it!
Branded it in me even though I couldn't see.
World had the enemy trying to fool me.
Take away what He gave & screw me.

He blessed me with this gift & I intend to do all I can with it!
Write words, split verbs & run with it!
Then get up & tell stories with the best of them.

Because in me is HIM
so there's no way I can't win!!
Knowing that in showing & giving love is not a sin!

So grab on to what HE gave you
Find it, mold it, think it, use it!!
Be like Old School Nike and Just Do It!
There's no way YOU can't win!

Remember 3 wise men came bearing gifts

& we've been receiving them ever since!!!

THIS NEXT PIECE IS A BONUS PEEK FROM THE UPCOMING BOOK ENTITILED:

THE ANGRY LESBIAN'S COLLECTION OF POEMS & INCREDIBLY SHORT STORIES

COLLARD GREENS & SUGAR CANE

Miss Sugar Cane looked good today. Her name is really not Miss Sugar Cane but Ms. Sally B. and she is the prettiest thing I ever seen. See people describe her as mean and surly, but I think I know Ms. Sally B.'s story. She is a gorgeous, beautiful lady and I just want to say hello to her every time I see her face.

She came over to me the other day and told me she was cooking a pot of collard greens, and she wanted a bit of that special seasoning my mama used to make, and didn't tell no one the recipe but me. So I know what Ms. Sally B. wanted, and I was hoping it was a taste of my sugar cane. I know something she don't think I do. See I have a crush on Ms. Sally B. and she act like she don't be seein' me… but I caught her looking at my booty the other day and, instead of me turning away I stayed and watched her linger over my big behind. I look in her eyes and she look at me, her head now down and bashful… and before she turns around I seen her glaze over in laughter in her spirit. It made me tickle.

The day came when it was time for me to taste her greens. I put in my secret seasoning my mama gave to me. Stirred the pot, made the water taste so good, and as she waited for the greens to cook down, I decided it was my time to give it a try. See Ms. Sally B. been watching me for a long time now… an I know in my heart I caught her eye.

I walk up to her and say, "Ms. Sally B., I see how you be looking at me" She spoke in a hard, harsh tone, "Girl, what you talkin' about, what do you mean??!!" "Ms. Sally B. I seen you watching my big ol' booty, you look at it up and down…" and before I could finish my sentence she flung her hand in the air and said;

“Go on Girl with that non-sense now!!!” “Ms. Sally B. you don’t scare me… I know what you want and what you need” Ms. Sally B. looked hard and mean, stood up and stared down at me. Her eyes I could tell she was pissed off, she was angry. I said, “don’t be mad at me, I just come over here to fix your greens. I don’t mean you no harm, but Ms. Sally B. I can’t help it… I want so badly to be in your arms.” Ms. Sally B. paused like she was thinking for a second before she yelled “Hush now Girl, I don’t need this mess…” and before she could utter another word I undid the first two buttons at the top of my dress. She looked at me hard and got silent no less.

I walked over to the pot of greens to give them a stir, and turned my booty in her direction with a slight seductive twirl. She just stood there silent looking at me. I turned toward her, unbuttoned the rest of my dress stepping slowly out of it as it dropped to the floor. Ms. Sally B. couldn’t take it anymore!

She said, “Baby girl, would you like a glass of lemonade?” “ See I have watched you many times… for many days.” “There is no way I can tell you how badly I wished to taste the sweetness of sugar cane between your legs!” “It’s hard right now for me to say, that at nights I wished you would come and stay.” “Yes the collard greens was my open door to let my eyes explore you more, of course now knowing you want me too….” She shook her head with a smile. “Have this glass of lemonade baby, the collard greens can wait, I want to make a meal out of you!”

Ms. Sally B. approached me slowly yet strong with a glass of ice cold lemonade in hand she fetched from the fridge. I remember the ice cubes clinking a little harder in the glass, that made me smile a little because under her smooth exterior she was nervous, maybe even scared.

I made sure I had on my new bright white panties and a crisp cotton bra. I had on those garters with the long stockings my mama told me never to wear, but I wanted to imagine Ms. Sally B.'s face seeing me in my underwear. Ms. Sally B. seemed to like it.....Ohhhhh Weeeee, Ms. Sally B. Ooooohhh! She touched my nipples nice and slow, then sucked my neck I knew a hickie would show! She rubbed my body down, then grabbed my big ol' asssss… Ms. Sally B.. Ms. Sally B! the things she said and did to me!! I never knew it could be so good. Ms. Sally B. cooked me collard greens every week after that, and told me every day if she could!

Unfortunately others in our neighborhood seemed ever curious and some even knowing. Started harassing us sun up till sun down every morning. They was calling us names, even had the nerve to throw things at us.
Sally B. came home one day with somethin' dead on her mattress!!

Our time together was over even though I adored her. Ms. Sally B. packed up bags and headed out to Memphis early this morning.

I love you Ms. Sally B.

Signed, Your Sweet Sugar Cane

ABOUT THE AUTHOR

Tina Cates, Poet name Dyvacat, started writing in her teenage years which consisted of poetry and songs. She later began an online poetry group that pushed her into expanding her poetry onto the stage. She has performed her pieces for Sappho's Return, Out Fest Film Festival, The Found Theatre in Long Beach, Ca. and several other venues across Southern Ca., New York and in Sacramento where she currently resides. She has been published in several books and online magazines.

She is the Author of Spoken Wordz and Kitty Kat Letters.

Look out for her 3rd book with a host of other great poets and writers coming soon from Glover Lane Publishing:

The Angry Lesbian's Collection of Poems & Incredibly Short Stories

www.ingramcontent.com/pod-product-compliance
Lightning Source LLC
LaVergne TN
LVHW020651100826
845148LV00012B/2423

* 9 7 8 0 6 1 5 6 5 4 0 1 0 *